JE 362.41
Car   Carter, Alden R.
             Seeing things my way

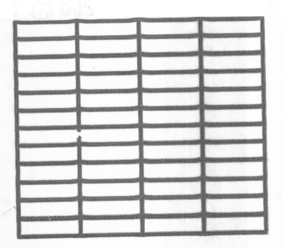

Avon Grove Free Library
11 Exchange Place
West Grove, PA 19390

DEMCO

Seeing Things My Way

Alden R. Carter
photographs by Carol S. Carter

Albert Whitman & Company
Morton Grove, Illinois

Library of Congress Cataloging-in-Publication Data
Carter, Alden R.
Seeing things my way/by Alden R. Carter;
    photographs by Carol S. Carter.
        p.   cm.
Summary: A second-grader describes how she and
    other students learn to use a variety of equipment
    and methods to cope with their visual impairments.
ISBN 0-8075-7296-9
        1. Visually handicapped children—Juvenile literature.
    2. Self-help devices for the disabled—Juvenile
    literature. [1. Visually handicapped. 2. Physically
    handicapped—Education. 3. Self-help devices for
    the disabled.] I. Carter, Carol S., ill. II. Title.
HV1596.3.C37 1998
362.4'183'083—dc21
        98-5893
CIP
AC

Text copyright © 1998 by Alden R. Carter.

Photographs copyright © 1998 by Carol S. Carter.

Published in 1998 by Albert Whitman & Company,
6340 Oakton Street, Morton Grove, Illinois 60053-2723.

Published simultaneously in Canada
by General Publishing, Limited, Toronto.

All rights reserved. No part of this book may be
    reproduced or transmitted in any form or by
    any means, electronic or mechanical, including
    photocopying, recording, or by any information
    storage and retrieval system, without permission
    in writing from the publisher.

Printed in the United States of America.
10 9 8 7 6 5 4 3 2 1
The design is by Pamela Kende.
The text typeface is Caslon.

The Braille shown on p. 15 is from *The Mangold
Developmental Program of Tactile Perception and Braille
Recognition, Teachers' Manual* by Sally Mangold
(Castro Valley, CA: Exceptional Teaching, 1994).

About the Author and Photographer

Alden R. Carter is the author of thirty-two
books for children and young adults,
including the celebrated novels *Dogwolf,
Up Country, Between a Rock and a Hard
Place,* and *Bull Catcher.* With his
daughter, Siri, he wrote *I'm Tougher
Than Asthma!,* an *American Bookseller*'s
"Pick of the Lists" selection for 1996.
He is also the author of *Big Brother
Dustin,* a University of Wisconsin-
Madison Cooperative Children's
Book Center (CCBC) *Choice* for 1997
and an *Oppenheim Toy Portfolio* Gold
Seal winner.

Carol S. Carter is a graduate of the Rocky
Mountain School of Photography
in Missoula, Montana. Her work has
appeared in several previous books
by her husband, Alden, including
Modern China and *The Battle of
Gettysburg.* She worked as photo
coordinator with photographer
Dan Young on *Big Brother Dustin.*

The Carters live in Marshfield, Wisconsin.

To the "tough cookies":

Amanda Coffren

Erin Bertz

Kali Luettgen

Nicky Bronson

David Hugo

Stacy Fuehrer

Many thanks to all who helped with *Seeing Things My Way*, especially Dawn, Jim, Naomi, and Serena Coffren; Linda, Phil, Tim, Dan, and Lindsay Bertz; Patty Chronquist and her students; Alice Kapla; Katherine Echola; Joan Doak; Robin Safford; Wendy Jones; Sherry Wick; Becky Ratts; Jeff Murray; David Berge; Diane Kleinschmidt; the Cai family; Don Olson and Melvin; Dr. James Nickerson; our children, Siri and Brian Carter; and the students and staff of Grant Elementary School, Marshfield, Wisconsin, and Grant Elementary School and Wausau West High School, Wausau, Wisconsin. Our particular thanks to Jim Gilmore, Karen Schultz, and our editor, Abby Levine.

I'm Amanda, and this is my friend Catherine. This is how she looks to you.

$\mathcal{A}$nd this is how she looks to me.

$\mathcal{T}$he missing places are called blind
spots. Glasses can't help, and I have a pair
mostly to protect my eyes. I lose my glasses
about three times a week, but Mom always
finds them. And I've found some really good
places to lose them, too!

I lost a lot of my sight because I was really sick when I was in kindergarten. I had a tumor, which is a lump that shouldn't be there, inside my head. The doctors took it out, and I had to go through some treatments that made me feel pretty awful. But they worked! Now every few months, my mom takes me to Dr. Nickerson so he can see how I'm doing. I'm fine, I tell him. But he checks me over anyway, which is OK, because he makes me laugh.

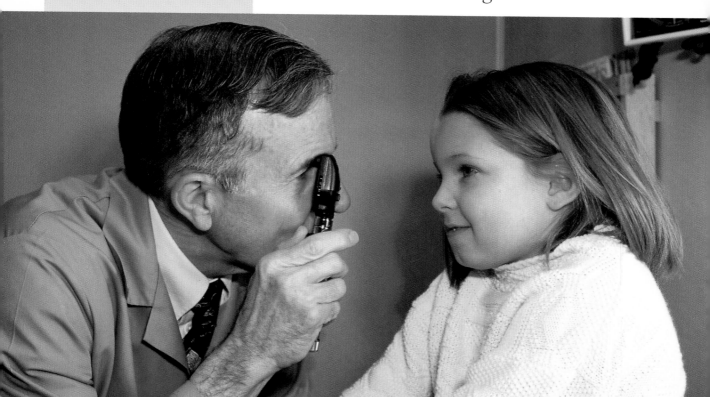

I was out of school for a long time and had to learn to read at home. My mom and dad got me a CCTV, which stands for Closed-Circuit Television. I can put a book or worksheet on my easel and then run the camera over it so the letters come up big on the screen.

*B*ecause I kept up at home, I was able to go to second grade this year with the other kids my age. It was a little scary going back, but I was mostly happy, especially when I found out that Mrs. Chronquist was going to be my teacher. And listen, first-graders—what kids say about her keeping a big, hairy spider in her desk drawer . . .

*W*ell, it's not true.

Really!

*T*here are other kids in school with vision impairments. My friend Erin was born almost blind in one eye and with very poor vision in the other. But she does fine in school, and she's about the fastest runner in our grade. (Almost as fast as me.) We have CCTVs, magnifiers, and big-print books to help us do our work. The other kids think the big-print books are especially cool!

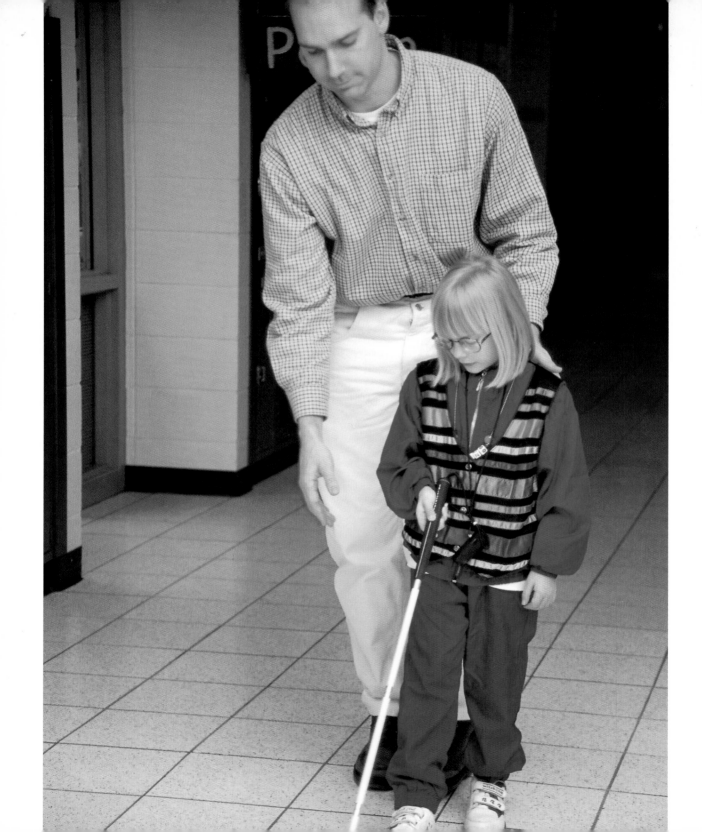

Twice a week, Mr. Gilmore, a special teacher for the visually impaired, comes to help us. He is showing Erin how to use a cane so she can find her way around strange places better. She's memorized her home and the school so well she can get around them with her eyes closed. I've seen her do it!

Erin's also practicing with a monocular so she can make out things farther away. This is how Erin sees a stop sign with and without her monocular. It's always blurry, but the monocular brings it a lot closer so that she can tell what it is.

$\mathcal{E}$rin's vision will probably stay pretty much the same, but someday I might lose more of mine. So Mr. Gilmore is helping me learn Braille (which rhymes with rail). Braille is a way for people with vision impairments to read. Each letter is made up of a group of raised dots that are read by touch. I've learned almost the whole alphabet, and soon I'm going to start reading simple stories.

𝓑raille was invented in 1829 by Louis Braille, a teacher in France. He lost his sight when he was three, but he always wanted to read. Today there are Braille magazines, newspapers, and whole libraries of books.

$\mathcal{M}$r. Gilmore is teaching me how to use a Brailler, which is a Braille typewriter. My friends Nicky and David, who are in fourth grade at another school, use Braillers to take notes in class and to answer worksheet questions. Nicky has only a little sight and David has none, but using Braille and Braillers they can keep up with their class.

Computers can be a big help for people
with vision impairments. My friend Kali,
who doesn't see at all, is using a program
that reads aloud what she types in. Mrs.
Schultz, who teaches visually impaired kids
at Kali's school, is giving her a spelling test.
Kali just got the word *pumpkin* right and
is very proud.

*E*very other day, I go to the physical therapist at our school. Because of the blind spots in my vision, I have problems with depth perception—which means I can't always tell how near or far away something is. People who have poor depth perception can also have trouble with balance. I practice by walking the balance beam and swinging on the tube. My balance has gotten so good that I've started ballet lessons!

After school, I play with my sisters, Naomi and Serena. Because I was sick for so long, I'm pretty small for my age. Naomi is taller than I am, even though she's two years younger. But I'm still the boss!

Thursday afternoon we go grocery shopping with my mom. As a treat, she lets us pick out something extra. This week it took us forever to decide if we wanted a pineapple, a mango, or something called a papaya. Mom finally said, "Oh, all right. Let's take all three."

I think Friday is the best day of the week. This Friday my friend Siri invited Erin and me to a slumber party. And there isn't anything better than a slumber party! We ate pizza, made necklaces, played telephone, and got popcorn in the bed.

After Siri's mom gave up telling us to go to sleep, we told scary stories until way past midnight.

*A*nd we weren't a bit tired in the morning!

Really!

Sunday night, after Naomi and Serena are in bed, I get some special time with my dad. It's good to sit in his lap and let him read books to me. A lot of times, I fall asleep before he finishes the first one.

$\mathcal{A}$nd the next thing I know, it's Monday morning and the sun is shining and I've got important things to do—like trying to figure out what necklace goes with my Green Bay Packer jersey.

Some kids have asked me if I feel bad about being vision-impaired. Well, I don't like it much. I mean, who would? But I don't have time to feel sorry for myself. I am *toooo* busy.

$\mathcal{M}$y mom says many famous people have had vision impairments: Louis Braille; the writer Helen Keller, who couldn't see *or* hear; the famous poets Homer and Milton; the singers Stevie Wonder and Ray Charles; and a bunch of others.

My hero is Stacy, who goes to high school in a town near my home. Stacy has been blind since birth, but she gets mostly A's, sings in the school choir, and plays flute in the band. When she talks to grade-schoolers about being blind, she reads them a story in Braille. Her fingers just fly across the page!

To read music, Stacy had to learn a different kind of Braille. Mrs. Schultz helps her memorize the music by playing each piece for her to hear.

*P*eople with visual impairments can do almost anything. They play cards and sports, go to the movies, take vacations, have families, and work at all sorts of jobs. When I feel like dancing, I can tune in WISM in Eau Claire, Wisconsin, and hear my favorite DJ, Don Olson. Don is blind, but that hasn't stopped him and his helping dog, Melvin, from having a show that really rocks!

I'm thankful for every day I can see. Don Olson lost his sight when he was five, and David, Kali, and Stacy have never seen at all. So I'm lucky. And if someday I lose more of my sight, I'm still going to be the star of my own life.

My dad says I'm one tough cookie. And you know something?

*H*e's right!

*A*nd my friends are pretty tough cookies, too.

I mean, *really!*